TASTE

The Flavors of Vidanta

❋ VIDANTA®

¡Saludos!

It is a great pleasure to share this collection of recipes from our kitchens with you and your family. Vidanta Dining started out with just a few small restaurants many years ago, but we've grown alongside the company, and now we have almost 50 different restaurants and bars at the Vidanta resorts.

We want dining to be an unforgettable part of your vacation, where you can try the finest cuisines from around the world — authentic Mexican, French, seafood, Asian, Italian, Spanish, Mediterranean, the flavors of the Yucatán, gourmet burgers — it's all made with the freshest ingredients and locally sourced whenever possible.

We're always asking ourselves, "What's next? How can we satisfy every palate, every expectation?" We've assembled an amazing team of chefs who bring their own style, creativity, and soul into the kitchen to create new concepts, new ideas, and new flavors.

I invite you to try one of these recipes at home. If it doesn't work out, you can always enjoy it on your next vacation — every Vidanta destination has its own unique restaurants and delicious dishes for you to savor.

Be sure to visit La Plaza in Vidanta Nuevo Vallarta where our Executive Chef, Cassandra Beretta, has put together a great collection of culinary delights like fine pastries and chocolates, artisan breads, house-cured meats, and gourmet prepared meals. And when you can, you must get to Vidanta Riviera Maya to experience the amazing dinner journey we created for JOYÀ, the Cirque du Soleil show.

From all the chefs, sous chefs, cooks, waiters, and hosts at Vidanta Dining, buen provecho!

Alexis Bostelmann
Vidanta Corporate Chef

Don't miss JOYÀ — a collaboration by Vidanta and Cirque du Soleil, and Cirque's first-ever culinary adventure.

The Flavors of Vidanta

Food has always done much more than fill the belly.

Food nurtures the soul, warms the heart, and brings people together in ways that nothing else can. And the dinner table has always been the place where we come together to share meals, stories, laughter, and even a few tears. It's where we have tough conversations and make future plans. As you read this, at dinner tables around the world, people are making time to reconnect with their loved ones. The littlest ones are fidgeting, waiting to be excused. The wisest ones are savoring every sip and every moment. This is where memories are made.

Behind all of this is the artful production we call cooking. This is where the senses collide in a beautiful symphony of colors, sounds, aromas, texture, and, of course, taste. The deep purple of the eggplant. Bright red cherry tomatoes. Chop, chop, chop! The snapping of crisp green beans. Garlic sizzling in oil. The sharp smell of fresh-cut peppers. Fresh bread baking in the oven. Slice, slice, slice! The clinking of silverware and plates. The chatter of conversation. What a beautiful and tasty affair!

The pages of Taste will take you on your own beautiful, tasty journey. You'll find some ingredients you've never used before and some flavors that stir the memory. These recipes are now yours to enjoy — the most popular dishes from the Vidanta restaurants.

At Vidanta, we say that we're "inspiring generations of happiness." We hope you use this cookbook over and over again, inspiring your guests, making everyone smile with each delicious bite.

Bookmark your favorites, dog-ear the pages, and wear out the spine. That will mean lots of memories are being made around your dinner table.

Savor every bite. Enjoy.

CONTENTS

Recipe on page 71

Giant Macaron

TRY THIS DISH
AT PUNTA ARENA
AT VIDANTA NUEVO
VALLARTA

APPETIZERS

Recipe on page 19

Spicy Tuna Tartare

YIELD
4 servings

PREP TIME
1 hour

COOK TIME
1 hr. 30 mins.

DIFFICULTY
intermediate

BURRATA

by Chef Alexis Bostelmann

Ingredients

For the leeks

- **2 large leeks,** with the white bulb cut in half to form 4 pieces
- **¾ cup** olive oil
- **1 ½ cups** chicken stock
- **6 slices** of lemon
- **5 thyme sprigs**
- Salt and pepper to taste

For the vinaigrette

- **3 tablespoons** old-style, whole grain mustard
- **¼ cup** olive oil
- **½ tablespoon** white wine vinegar
- **2 tablespoons** lime juice
- Stock, reserved from cooking leeks
- **4 shallots**, finely chopped
- **⅛ teaspoon** tarragon
- **½ teaspoon** sugar
- Salt and pepper to taste

For the fried leeks

- **1 leek**, julienned
- **1 tablespoon** all-purpose flour
- **1 cup** canola oil
- Salt and pepper to taste

For plating

- 4 each burrata cheese
- Beet sprouts (optional)

Directions

Leeks

Preheat oven to 350 ˚F (180 ˚C), place leeks, olive oil, and chicken stock in a baking dish. Add the rest of ingredients. Season with salt and pepper. Cover with aluminum foil and bake for 45 minutes. Remove from oven, uncover, cool, and reserve the cooking liquid. Reserve the lemons slices.

Vinaigrette

In a bowl, place mustard, stir continuously and add the olive oil, white wine vinegar, lime juice, the stock reserved from cooking the leeks, and the rest of the ingredients. Season with salt and pepper.

Fried leeks

Preheat the oil in a deep frying pan. Dredge leeks in flour. Add salt and pepper. Remove excess flour and deep-fry.

To serve

Place hot baked leeks on a plate. On top of the leeks, place the burrata cheese and drizzle with the vinaigrette. Decorate with the fried leeks and a slice of the reserved lemons.

YIELD
4 servings

PREP TIME
45 minutes

DIFFICULTY
beginner

CAMPECHANA

by Chef Mario López

Ingredients

For the cocktail

- **2 teaspoons** clarified butter
- **4 large** scallops
- **12** 26/30 cooked shrimps
- **7 ounces (200 g)** cooked octopus
- Salt and pepper to taste

For the chili pepper vinaigrette

- **6 tablespoons** lime juice
- **10** spicy piquín chili peppers (small)
- **10 tablespoons** olive oil
- Salt to taste

To serve

- **1 green onion**, with no leaves, blanched, and separated into layers
- **1 cucumber**, peeled, and thinly sliced
- Microgreens (optional)

Directions

Cocktail

Season the scallops with salt and pepper, heat the clarified butter in a sauté pan and sear the scallops. Cut the scallops in 2 pieces and the cooked octopus into 1½ inch (2 cm) cubes.

Chili pepper vinaigrette

In a blender, purée the lime juice, piquín chili peppers, and olive oil. Season with salt. Strain and reserve.

To serve

In a bowl, mix together seafood, vinaigrette, cucumber slices, and green onion. Add salt if needed. Serve in a dish and drizzle with more vinaigrette. Decorate with microgreens.

Chef Mario López's Tip: When blanching vegetables or herbs, the water must be salty enough to keep the natural colors, enhance the flavors, and prevent them from losing mineral salts during cooking. Chilling them immediately in iced water will stop the cooking and keep them looking fantastic.

YIELD
4 servings

PREP TIME
45 minutes

DIFFICULTY
beginner

YELLOW CEVICHE
by Chef Concepción Gonzaga

Ingredients

For the ceviche and sweet potato crisps

- **5 ounces (160 g)** octopus, cooked
- **5 ounces (160 g)** fresh salmon
- **5 ounces (160 g)** scallops
- **5 ounces (160 g)** grouper
- **2 ounces (50 g)** cherry tomatoes, cut in halves
- **2 tablespoons** green onion, green part, chopped
- **2 tablespoons** red onion, julienned
- **2 tablespoons** cilantro sprigs, chopped
- **4** cilantro sprigs, for decoration
- **4 tablespoons** sweet potatoes, julienned
- Frying oil
- Salt and pepper to taste

For the sauce

- **3 ½ tablespoons** yellow aji chili pepper paste
- **1 cup** sweet lime juice
- **1 cup** lime juice
- **1 tablespoon** honey
- **1** garlic clove
- **2 tablespoons** olive oil
- Salt and pepper to taste

Directions

Ceviche and sweet potato crisps

Cut salmon, grouper, octopus, and scallops in ½-inch (1-cm) cubes. Mix in a bowl with salt and pepper. Reserve and refrigerate. Heat oil and deep-fry julienned sweet potatoes. Strain, remove excess oil with paper towels, and season with salt. Reserve.

Sauce

In a bowl, mix the yellow aji chili pepper paste, both lime juices, and honey. Add garlic and olive oil. Process in a blender.

To serve

In a bowl, mix fish, seafood, vegetables, and sauce. Season with salt and pepper and serve. Top each ceviche with the sweet potato crisps.

YIELD
4 servings

PREP TIME
30 minutes

DIFFICULTY
beginner

SPICY TUNA TARTARE

by Chef Jorge Ildefonso

Ingredients

For the tartare

- **21 ounces (600 g)** fresh, sushi-grade tuna
- **3 tablespoons** olive oil
- **2 tablespoons** sesame oil
- **2 tablespoons** red onion, minced
- **½** garlic clove, minced
- **1** lemon for juice and zest
- **1** sprig of cilantro, finely chopped

For the spicy soy sauce

- **3** serrano chili peppers
- **1 teaspoon** corn oil
- **1 tablespoon** ginger, chopped
- **½ cup** soy sauce
- **3 tablespoons** lime juice

To serve

- Banana leaves for decoration
- **1** cucumber, cut in fine half moons
- **4** wonton leaves
- Oil for frying
- **1** avocado
- Microgreens and edible flowers (optional)

Directions

Tartare

Cut the tuna in ½ inch cubes. Add two tablespoons olive oil, sesame oil, minced onion and garlic, grated lemon zest, and two tablespoons of freshly squeezed lemon juice. Blend thoroughly and add half a sprig of finely chopped cilantro. Season with salt and pepper.

Spicy soy sauce

Slice serrano chili peppers and sauté with the minced ginger, the soy sauce, and the lime juice using a little bit of oil. Reserve.

To serve

Cut a banana leaf in 4 long strips for decoration and place them at the bottom of the plate. Place the sliced cucumber on top and serve the tartare on top of these (in the picture, we use a small mold to achieve the shape). Fry the wonton leaves, decorate with avocado segments and the sprouts. Serve with the fried wontons and the spicy soy sauce on the side.

VIDANTA CORPORATE CHEF

Alexis Bostelmann

For twelve years as Vidanta's Corporate Chef, Chef Alexis Bostelmann has been imagining and implementing new concepts for restaurants and new recipes for signature dishes. His creative vision has helped give Vidanta Dining its distinctive identity. "One of my jobs is to take traditional dishes and create new ones using different ingredients and flavors, such as the lobster risotto with bacon at Tramonto or the coconut shrimp at Havana Moon," he explains. Just like other chefs, he first became fascinated with cooking as a child helping his parents cook in their home in Mexico City. When he discovered that cooking was an art, Alexis devoted his life to it.

During his impressive international career, Alexis has prepared meals for several heads of state, celebrities, and other illustrious individuals staying at the resort, but even now, at the height of his career, he continues to be very humble. He simply wants to cook good food and create memorable culinary experiences for members. Always the mentor of younger chefs, Alexis notes, "Those who want to be part of this profession need dedication, passion, and patience. Before entering the culinary world, learn about it because often people think it is a glamorous world. Sometimes it is, but it also entails sacrifice. But enjoying what you do is the greatest reward."

"I rarely cook for myself. The real satisfaction comes when you see the pleasure other people get from your cooking!"

TRY THIS DISH AT EPAZOTE AT VIDANTA NUEVO VALLARTA

SOUPS & SALADS

Recipe on page 31

Black Bean Soup

YIELD
4 servings

PREP TIME
2 hrs. 30 mins.

COOK TIME
2 hours

DIFFICULTY
intermediate

WHITE POZOLE

by Chef Daniel Hernández

Ingredients

For the pozole

- **1.1 pounds (½ kg)** pork bones
- **½ pound (¼ kg)** pork Boston butt, cut in four equal pieces
- **1** white medium onion
- **1** clove
- **3** bay leaves
- **2.6 quarts (2 ½ l)** water
- **7 ounces (200 g)** pre-cooked hominy
- **1 teaspoon** oregano
- Salt to taste

For the garnish

- **1** avocado
- **4** limes
- **8** corn tostadas (deep-fried tortillas)
- **4** red radishes, thinly sliced
- **8** leaves of washed romaine lettuce, finely julienned
- **4 teaspoons** oregano
- **4 teaspoons** chile de arbol chili peppers, dried and crushed
- **4 tablespoons** serrano chili pepper, finely chopped
- **4 tablespoons** fresh cilantro, chopped
- **1 tablespoon** onion, chopped
- Salt and pepper to taste

Directions

Pozole

Thoroughly wash bones with water. Place them in a large pot with previously-cut Boston butt into four equal pieces. Add onion, clove, bay leaves, water, and some salt. Bring to a boil and simmer for 1 ½ hours. Remove meat and shred. Add hominy, half of the oregano, and cook for 30 minutes more. Remove and discard bones, bay leaves, clove, and onion from the stock. Return the shredded pork to the stock and add the remaining oregano.

To serve

Serve the stock very hot with the hominy and the meat. Garnish with the lettuce on top, radishes, and a fan-shaped piece of avocado. Accompany with tostadas, oregano, lime wedges, chile de arbol chili pepper, onion, serrano chili pepper, and chopped cilantro.

Chef Daniel Hernández's Tip: Enjoy with a shot of mezcal (distilled alcoholic beverage made from maguey plant) and worm salt to enhance digestion.

YIELD
4 servings

PREP TIME
45 minutes

COOK TIME
15 minutes

DIFFICULTY
beginner

GREEN CHILI CREAM SOUP

by Chef Neftalí Ponce

Ingredients

For the cream soup
- **5** Anaheim chili peppers
- **1 ½ cups** milk
- **1** garlic clove
- **1** white onion
- **1** bay leaf
- **1** clove
- **1 pinch** nutmeg

- **2 tablespoons** butter
- **1 small** celery stalk, chopped
- **2 tablespoons** all-purpose flour
- **1 ½ cups** chicken stock
- **4 teaspoons** whipping cream
- **2 tablespoons** cream cheese
- Salt and pepper to taste

To serve
- **1 tablespoon** butter
- **3 tablespoons** corn kernels
- **1** garlic clove, minced
- **4 tablespoons** Caborca (region in Northern Mexico) cheese, cut in ½ inch (1 cm) cubes
- Sprouts for decoration (optional)
- Salt and pepper to taste

Directions

Green chili cream soup

Roast chili peppers over direct fire, turning to roast them uniformly. Wash all 5 chili peppers under running water, removing the black skin, seeds, white sections inside, and the stem. Reserve one pepper and cut into strips, for final decoration. Heat milk without boiling, add one garlic clove, ¼ onion, bay leaf, clove, salt and pepper, and a pinch of grated nutmeg. Cook for 3 minutes and strain. Place butter in a saucepan at high heat, add celery, garlic, and remaining onion cut into 3/4 in (2 cm.) pieces. Sauté, add flour, and cook until it turns a light golden color. Add roasted and peeled green chili pepper. Add the chicken stock and hot milk. Simmer for 12 minutes. Stir constantly. Purée in blender, adding the whipping cream, and cream cheese. Heat again in a saucepan, season to taste and serve.

To serve

Sauté corn kernels with butter and minced garlic. Add the remaining chili pepper strips. Add salt and pepper. Place cheese cubes in the center of the plate, add chili strips with corn and pour in hot cream soup. Decorate with sprouts, if desired.

Chef Neftalí Ponce's Tip: *Preferably use artisanal fresh cheese; its flavor is richer and goes perfectly with green chili soup.*

YIELD
4 servings

PREP TIME
1 hour

COOK TIME
1 hour

DIFFICULTY
intermediate

ROASTED BEET SALAD

by Chef Francisco Vargas

Ingredients

For the roasted beets
- **4** beets
- **4** avocado leaves
- **4** thyme sprigs
- **4 tablespoons** olive oil
- Salt and pepper to taste

For the caramelized pecans
- **4 tablespoons** toasted pecans
- **2 tablespoons** sugar

For the orange and chili peppers vinaigrette
- **1 cup** orange juice
- **2 teaspoons** lime juice
- **1 ½ teaspoons** honey
- **1** guajillo chili pepper, julienned
- **1** cascabel chili pepper, julienned
- **1 ½ tablespoons** Dijon mustard
- **¼ cup** apple cider vinegar
- **⅓ cup** olive oil
- Salt and pepper to taste

To serve
- **2** radishes
- **2** limes, juiced
- **2** oranges
- **8 tablespoons** fresh cheese, crumbled Feta or Queso Fresco
- **4 ounces (100 g)** blend of organic greens
- Beet sprouts (optional)

Directions

Roasted beets

Preheat oven to 400 ˚F (200 ˚C). Place one previously washed beet on a piece of aluminum foil with avocado leaf, thyme, olive oil, salt, and pepper. Fully wrap the beet with the foil and repeat for the rest of the beets. Bake for 25 minutes, open the foil and bake for 10 minutes more. Remove beets from the oven and let them cool. Peel the skin and then cut into half moons. Reserve cold.

Carmelized pecans

Place sugar in a pot with water, just enough to moisten the sugar. Bring to a boil at medium-high heat and melt the sugar until it is amber in color. Add the previously toasted pecans and stir constantly until caramelized. Remove from the heat, spread out, and let cool.

Orange and chili peppers vinaigrette

Place the orange juice in a small saucepan, together with the lime juice, honey, and chili peppers. Bring to a boil at medium heat and reduce half the liquid. Strain through a fine mesh strainer pressing the chili pepper pulp. Cool immediately. Add mustard, vinegar, olive oil and season to taste. Thinly slice the radishes, soak in remaining lime juice for 15 seconds. Peel the orange and section. Reserve.

To serve

On a plate, form a bed with lettuce that has been previously drizzled with the vinaigrette and seasoned with salt and pepper. Add the half moons of beet, orange segments, caramelized pecans, fresh cheese, radishes, and beet sprouts, and drizzle with more vinaigrette.

YIELD
4 servings

PREP TIME
45 minutes

COOK TIME
25 minutes

DIFFICULTY
beginner

BLACK BEAN SOUP

by Chef Enrique García

Ingredients

For the black bean soup

- **2 cups** black beans (soaked for 24 hours)
- **1** medium onion, in pieces
- **2** garlic cloves
- **3** epazote sprigs
- **2** cups milk
- **3 tablespoons** butter
- Salt and pepper to taste

To serve

- **1** avocado
- **4 tablespoons** Queso Fresco, cut into cubes
- **½** plantain (optional)
- **2** corn tortillas, cut in fine julienne
- Frying oil
- **4** epazote leaves
- **1 teaspoon** pasilla chili pepper
- Salt to taste

Directions

Bean cream soup

Cook beans until soft with abundant water, including onion, garlic, and an epazote sprig. Remove the epazote and purée in a blender and reserve. In a saucepan, heat the milk with butter. Pour in blended beans and simmer for 10 minutes, stirring constantly until it has a creamy consistency. Remove from the heat and strain. Place back on burner for 3 minutes. Add remaining epazote sprigs and season to taste.

To serve

Crush plantain and form 12 marble-size spheres. Heat the oil in a saucepan and fry the plantain spheres. Remove and drain. Fry tortilla strips. Remove, drain, and season with salt. Cut the avocado into cubes. Place the cheese and avocado at the bottom of the bowl. Add the cream soup and top with fried tortilla strips and fried plantain spheres. Decorate with an epazote sprig and the ground pasilla chili pepper.

Chef Enrique García's Tip: Preferably use artisanal fresh cheese because its flavor is richer and goes perfectly with the creamy bean soup.

EXECUTIVE CHEF, VIDANTA MAZATLÁN

Mario López

L'avenue du Mont-Royal and its culinary tradition led Mario López to his current role as Executive Chef at Vidanta Mazatlán. He was 20 years old, living in Montreal, when he started to sample different cuisines and fell in love with cooking. He's now an Executive Chef with a serious style — he respects tradition but likes to add his own touch to recipes to create innovative new tastes. He also favors fresh, regional products, grown and produced in an artisanal or traditional manner, "the old-fashioned way," he says with a smile.

He has adapted more dishes than he has created, but he believes that in both cases, the dish reflects the chef's style and personality. He admires American chef Thomas Keller, for his perfection, and Argentinean chef Francis Mallmann, for his authenticity. The food he enjoys the most is home cooking, because "cooking for those we love is giving love," he explains. He enjoys a light beer with ceviche, or a glass of red wine with a pizza slice from a wood-burning oven. And what does he think it takes to be a good chef? "Talent. But above all, love. The 'Chef' title is not earned in a university or in your parents' business, but through long hours, courage, determination, and effort."

"It was after trying so many varied flavors and textures of elaborate dishes that I began to fall in love with this profession."

EXECUTIVE CHEF, VIDANTA LOS CABOS

Francisco Vargas

A lover of home-cooked food, Francisco Vargas' specialty dish is his grandfather's recipe for cochinita pibil (Yucatan pork baked in banana leaves). Since he was a child, the Vidanta Los Cabos Executive Chef has identified himself with the kitchen — a place where he spent hours and hours with his mother, grandmother, and aunts preparing food. His style is a combination of classical and modern, with a pinch of spontaneity and a touch of originality.

An admirer of Mexican chef Enrique Olvera, he has created several original recipes. His favorite utensil is the chef's knife and his preferred condiments are basil and fresh ginger "because of the aroma and flavors they impart." Vargas also enjoys lunch or dinner with wine, either fruity whites or a Cabernet, but also enjoys fresh cocktails, like the virgin mojito. He believes that those who want to become a chef need to truly enjoy preparing meals. "Cooking is a pleasure and you should feel proud of knowing that someone else will enjoy it." Passionate and knowledgeable, Vargas says, "the first impression is through our eyes, and as a chef, one has to pay close attention to every single detail."

"I get carried away by instinct. I start with something in mind, but as I'm creating, I make changes."

TRY THIS DISH
AT GONG AT VIDANTA
RIVIERA MAYA

ENTRÉE - SKY

Recipe on page 41
Peking Duck

YIELD
4 servings

PREP TIME
1 hour

COOK TIME
1 hour

DIFFICULTY
intermediate

DUCK MAGRET

by Chef Cassandra Beretta

Ingredients

For the duck and asparagus

- **4** duck breasts
- **1 teaspoon** canola oil
- **16** asparagus spears
- **1 teaspoon** butter
- Salt and pepper to taste
- Microgreens and edible flowers (optional)

For the cauliflower purée

- **1** small cauliflower
- **2 tablespoons** canola oil
- **4 teaspoons** butter
- **3** garlic cloves

For the sauce

- **2** shallots, chopped
- **1** garlic clove, chopped
- **1 teaspoon** brown sugar
- **1 teaspoon** cardamom
- **½ cup** Port wine
- **1 cup** duck stock
- **2 tablespoons** butter
- Salt and pepper to taste

Directions

Duck and asparagus

Make crosscuts on the fat side of the duck breasts and season with salt and pepper. In a sauté pan with canola oil, sear the duck breasts for 2 minutes, fat side first. Turn them and sear for 2 minutes more. Cook in the oven for 7-8 minutes. The center must have a pink color. Serve the purée with the asparagus, the duck breast, and the sauce. For the asparagus, bring salted water in a saucepan to a boil. Cook the asparagus for 3-5 minutes and transfer to a bowl of iced water. Once cold, drain. Sauté the asparagus with butter, salt and pepper.

Cauliflower purée

Preheat the oven at 350 ˚F (180˚C). Chop the cauliflower into big pieces, season with salt and pepper, add oil and 2 teaspoons of butter. Put them into a baking pan. Roast in the oven with the garlic cloves for 25-30 minutes. Do not over roast the cauliflower: the color must be pale and the texture tender. Purée the cauliflower with the garlic until smooth. In a sauté pan, heat the purée with 2 teaspoons of butter, nutmeg, and cream. Season to taste.

Sauce

In a saucepan, heat 1 teaspoon of butter with shallots and garlic. Add brown sugar, cardamom, and Port wine. Reduce the Port wine until ¼ cup remains. Add the duck stock and simmer until ½ cup remains. Season to taste. Before serving, add 1 teaspoon of butter and whisk gently.

YIELD
4 servings

PREP TIME
2 hours

COOK TIME
1 hr. 30 mins.

DIFFICULTY
expert

PEKING DUCK

by Chef Gualberto Vázquez

Ingredients

For the duck marinade
- **One 5 pound (1 - 2.2 kg)** whole duck
- **½ tablespoon** Ajinomoto
- **½ tablespoon** ground black pepper
- **½ tablespoon** five spices powder
- **1 tablespoon** salt
- **2 tablespoons** white wine

For the glazing
- **1 cup** dark soy sauce
- **1 cup** honey
- **1 cup** hoisin sauce

- **1 cup** balsamic vinegar
- **3 cups** water
- **2 cups** sugar

For the stir fry
- **1 tablespoon** canola oil
- **1** garlic clove, finely chopped
- **1 tablespoon** fresh ginger, finely chopped
- **¼ cup** bamboo shoots
- **¼ cup** broccoli
- **½** zucchini, cut in half slices
- **½** onion, chopped
- **¼** cup mushrooms, cut in quarters
- **¼** cup snow peas, cooked
- **¼ cup** cauliflower

- **4** baby corn, cut in halves
- **6** bok choy leaves, cut in thick strips
- **½** carrot, cut in half slices
- **3 tablespoons** shiitake mushrooms, cut in strips
- **1 tablespoon** white wine
- **½ cup** chicken stock
- **½ teaspoon** Ajinomoto
- **1 tablespoon** sugar
- **1 tablespoon** soy sauce
- **1 tablespoon** oyster sauce
- **1 tablespoon** dark soy sauce
- **1 tablespoon** hoisin sauce
- **1 tablespoon** corn starch
- **1 tablespoon** sesame seed oil

Directions

Duck marinade

Mix all marinade ingredients until they form a paste. Rub the inside of the duck with this paste. Hang the duck from the chest with a hook. In a large pot with boiling water, taking the hook with your hand, pour water gently onto the bird with a ladle. Repeat 3 times. This will facilitate better glazing. Repeat 2 times, letting the bird dry for a few minutes in between. Mix all the glaze ingredients and heat them up in large saucepan in order to glaze the bird in the same way. Hang the duck in front of a fan and let dry for 24 hours. Preheat the oven to 300 ˚F (150 ˚C). Roast duck, breast facing up, for 40 minutes. Increase the temperature to 340 ˚F (170 ˚C) and continue roasting for 15 minutes. Let the bird rest for 10 minutes before serving. Make crosscut slices on the breasts and set aside.

Stir-fry

Bone the remaining duck and cut the meat in big pieces. In a pot with salted boiling water, cook vegetables for 1 minute and strain. In a sauté pan, heat canola oil and cook garlic, ginger, and vegetables. Add white wine and reduce until dry, pour in chicken broth and remaining ingredients (except for sesame oil and corn starch). Simmer for 1 minute, add cornstarch and cook until the sauce is uniform in consistency. Finish with sesame oil.

EXECUTIVE CHEF, VIDANTA NUEVO VALLARTA
AND VIDANTA PUERTO VALLARTA

Cassandra Beretta

Curiosity is a constant for Cassandra Beretta, Executive Chef of our largest development, Vidanta Nuevo Vallarta. She likes to figure out "the why" of every element in a dish and is an avid reader of every culinary book she can get her hands on. Food is her passion. She has an amazing ability to go from one kitchen to another with one single thing in mind: making sure members enjoy the best. "I like to create, to pay attention to detail, and to season every dish to perfection so it will always be a pleasure for our members," she says. This attention to detail is evident in the gourmet offerings at La Plaza at Vidanta Nuevo Vallarta. Cassandra worked with international chefs and sommeliers to create a culinary shopping experience where members can find everything from house-made pâté and cheeses, to fine pastries and artisan breads.

As a child, Cassandra started cooking very early, showing her natural talent at the summer cooking classes where her mother sent her every year. As the youngest in a group of adults, she stood out. "I remember one bakery course where I was the only child in a class of adults." Her education was also very focused towards the arts, which she credits with fostering her creativity. "I grew up visiting museums, dancing ballet for many years, painting, listening to opera, taking music lessons, and going to concerts. But the true way of expressing myself has always been in the kitchen."

"Cooking is a profession with a gift. To see the result of our work, all we have to do is look at the guest's expression after the first bite."

TRY THIS DISH
AT BAKAL AT VIDANTA
PUERTO PEÑASCO

ENTRÉE - LAND

Recipe on page 51

Beef Tenderloin

YIELD
4 servings

PREP TIME
1 hour

COOK TIME
15 minutes

DIFFICULTY
beginner

BEEF KEBABS

by Chef Felipe Hernández

Ingredients

For the kebabs

- **30 ounces (850 g)** good quality ground beef
- **5 tablespoons** red onion, chopped
- **1 teaspoon** garlic, minced
- **3 tablespoons** spearmint, chopped
- **2 teaspoons** cumin powder
- **2 teaspoons** paprika
- **1 teaspoon** coriander, ground
- **2 eggs**

- **¼ cup** panko breadcrumbs
- **6 tablespoons** olive oil
- Salt and pepper to taste
- **8** skewers, 6 inches long (15 cm)

For tzatziki

- **½ cup** natural yogurt, unsweetened
- **¼ cup** sour cream
- **2 teaspoons** lime juice
- **3 tablespoons** cucumber, cut into small cubes
- **1 teaspoon** dill, chopped

- **½ teaspoon** garlic, finely minced
- Salt and pepper to taste

To serve

- **3 tablespoons** red wine vinegar
- **1 teaspoon** Dijon mustard
- **1 pinch** oregano
- **5 tablespoon** olive oil
- **4** Campari tomatoes, quartered
- **½** yellow pepper, cut into cubes
- **½** green pepper, cut into cubes
- **2 teaspoons** black olives, sliced
- **⅛** onion, thinly sliced
- **1 cup** mixed greens, washed
- **4 tablespoons** Feta cheese, cut into cubes
- Salt and pepper to taste

Directions

Kebabs

In a bowl, mix the ground beef with onions, garlic, and spearmint. Add cumin, paprika, coriander, panko breadcrumbs, 4 tablespoons of olive oil, and eggs. Season with salt and pepper. Form 24 meatballs of the same size. Take 3 meatballs and insert a skewer to form a kebab. Repeat process with the rest of the meatballs. Add salt and pepper to the kebabs, then cook in a hot skillet with the rest of the olive oil. Reserve.

Tzatziki

Blend natural yogurt, cream, and lime juice in a bowl. Add cucumber cut into cubes, chopped dill, and garlic. Season to taste.

To serve

Blend vinegar, mustard, oregano, and olive oil. Season with salt and pepper and reserve. In a bowl, mix Campari tomatoes, peppers, olives, red onion, and greens. Season with salt and pepper, pour into vinaigrette, add Feta cheese, and mix ingredients well. Serve kebabs with Greek salad and tzatziki on the side.

YIELD
4 servings

PREP TIME
2 hrs. 30 mins.

COOK TIME
1 hr. 30 mins.

DIFFICULTY
intermediate

COCHINITA PIBIL

by Chef Enrique Garcia

Ingredients

For the cochinita
- **2.2 pounds (1 kg)** cooked ham
- **½ pound (¼ kg)** Boston butt pork
- **8 tablespoons** pork lard
- **200 g (.4 lb)** annatto paste
- **1 cup** sour orange juice
- **¼ teaspoon** cumin powder
- **1 teaspoon** dry oregano
- **1 teaspoon** white pepper powder
- **½ teaspoon** black pepper powder
- **½ teaspoon** cinnamon powder
- **3** black peppercorns, coarsely ground
- **3** garlic cloves
- **2** guajillo chili peppers, seeded
- Salt and pepper to taste

For the marinated onion
- **1** small red onion
- **4 tablespoons** white vinegar
- **2 tablespoons** lime juice
- **1** habanero chili pepper
- **½ teaspoon** oregano
- Salt and pepper to taste

For the fried plantains
- **1** plantain, ripe
- **1 teaspoon** all-purpose flour
- Oil for frying
- Salt and pepper to taste

To serve
- Tortillas (preferably handmade)
- **4** cilantro sprigs
- **4** banana leaves, cut into circles (optional)

Directions

Cohinita

Preheat oven to 300 ˚F (150 ˚C) and place banana leaves on a baking dish. Cut pork into medium-sized pieces, season with salt and pepper, and rub with pork lard. In a blender, process annatto paste, sour orange juice, cumin, oregano, both peppers, peppercorns, garlic, and guajillo chili peppers. Adjust seasoning with salt. Place meat on the dish and baste with the adobo sauce. Bake for 90 minutes.

Marinated onion

Finely julienne the red onion. Add white vinegar and lime juice. Add chopped habanero chili pepper and oregano. Season with salt and pepper and reserve.

Fried plantains

Cut plantain in ¼ inch (½ cm.) slices. Add salt and pepper. Dredge in flour and deep-fry in hot oil. Drain and reserve.

To serve

Serve with the marinated onion, tortilla, and deep-fried plantain slices. Decorate with a cilantro sprig and the banana leaf.

YIELD
4 servings

PREP TIME
45 minutes

COOK TIME
45 minutes

DIFFICULTY
beginner

BEEF TENDERLOIN

by Chef Neftalí Ponce

Ingredients

For the beef tenderloin and sauce
- **4** filet mignon, **7 ounces (200 g)** each
- **½ tablespoon** olive oil
- **2 tablespoons** butter
- **½ cup** Bacanora liquor
- **1 cup** veal demi-glace
- **2 tablespoons** heavy cream
- **4** rosemary sprigs
- Salt and pepper to taste

Roasted potatoes and asparagus
- **3** guajillo chili peppers, seeded
- **1** garlic clove
- **¼** white onion
- **1** bay leaf
- **1** thyme sprig
- **1** clove
- **12** spring potatoes
- **2 tablespoons** olive oil
- **20** asparagus
- **4** bacon strips
- Mesquite smoked salt
- Salt and pepper to taste

Directions

Beef tenderloin and sauce

Marinate the beef tenderloins with salt, pepper, olive oil, and butter. Heat a sauté pan and cook beef for 2 minutes per side. Flambé with the Bacanora liquor and reduce until dry. Add demi-glace and continue cooking until desired degree of doneness is achieved. Remove the filets and keep warm. In the same sauté pan, add the cream and cook for 3 minutes. Season to taste.

Roasted potatoes and asparagus

In a saucepan with a small amount of water, cook the guajillo chili peppers, one garlic clove, onion, bay leaf, thyme sprig, clove, salt, and pepper for 5 minutes. Purée in a blender and strain. Cook potatoes until soft in salted water, chill them in ice water and strain. Rub potatoes with guajillo sauce. Season with salt and pepper. Add olive oil and roast until golden brown in a sauté pan. Rub asparagus with olive oil, smoked salt, and pepper. Cook them on the grill. Prepare 4 bouquets of asparagus with 5 spears each by wrapping with bacon strips. Sear bouquet in a sauté pan on all sides to ensure bacon is cooked.

To serve

Serve the sauce on the bottom of the dish, place the filet mignon on top and accompany with the potatoes and asparagus. Decorate with rosemary.

EXECUTIVE CHEF, VIDANTA PUERTO PEÑASCO

Neftalí Ponce

The "Iron Chef" of Puerto Peñasco, Neftalí Ponce, became a chef by a strange twist of fate. After evaluating his choices, Neftalí Ponce studied hotel management and culinary arts. He then approached the hotel where his father worked as a taxi driver where he landed his first job. "From that time to now, I am still in the kitchen," he says.

Throughout his career, Neftalí has had the pleasure of cooking for top politicians, the Mexican soccer team, and pop singer Luis Miguel. His favorite condiment is basil "because it is versatile, and can be used to flavor anything from an entrée to a dessert or beverage." His hobbies are those of a simple man and loves food "made with love, my mother's food, or just simply some refried beans!" Traveling with his mortar and pestle is a reality for him, but winning first place in the Iron Chef competition in Puerto Peñasco demonstrated that cooking is not an easy profession, but one that is rewarding. "It is a great satisfaction when a guest leaves the plate empty."

"When you cook, you truly become an artist, since your creativity is reflected in every dish. You have to love what you do."

EXECUTIVE CHEF, VIDANTA RIVIERA MAYA

Francisco Llil

According to Mexican chef Francisco Llil, it takes three virtues to be a chef —
passion, patience, and discipline. As the Executive Chef at Vidanta Riviera Maya, he
applies all three to his craft and tells this to everyone who wants to start a career
among pots and pans. His cooking mentor was Iñaki Aguirre from the Basque
Country, the famous Spanish region that heavily influenced his cooking style and
preferences. He has a fondness for using Mediterranean ingredients, especially
olive oil, garlic, and seafood. "I worked with mentors from the North Atlantic, and I
have constantly cooked fish and shellfish. But over the last 20 years, I have been in
different countries and all of that makes you eclectic. It allows you to see what is new
and adapt a traditional recipe to make it more contemporary," he explains.

Francisco goes back to the basics, reinterprets recipes, and creates a new way to say
things with food. "I like the contrast of textures, the fact that you find sizzling tastes
here and there, and that you can make a visual impact with colors and shapes.
They say that love is perceived first through the eyes."

"Garlic gives a lot of personality to whatever you are cooking. It goes well with meat, fish, and pasta, but I cannot think of it without olive oil. That is a true marriage!"

TRY THIS DISH AT SAMBA, CAFÉ DEL LAGO, & BALCHÉ AT VIDANTA ACAPULCO

ENTRÉE - SEA

Recipe on page 63
Sea Bass Filet

YIELD
4 servings

PREP TIME
1 hr. 20 mins.

COOK TIME
1 hr. 30 mins.

DIFFICULTY
expert

PAELLA VALENCIANA

by Chef Javier Loyola

Ingredients

For the paella
- **4 tablespoons** olive oil
- **7 ounces (200 g)** chicken breast, cut in cubes
- **1** chorizo sausage, sliced
- **14 ounces (400 g)** paella rice
- **4 cups** lobster or shrimp stock
- **8** pork baby back ribs, cooked
- **12** shrimp, head on
- **12** calamari rings
- **8 tablespoons** green peas
- **12** mussels
- Salt and pepper to taste

For the saffron-white wine and vegetables
- **½ box** saffron
- **½ cup** white wine
- **½** red bell pepper
- **½** yellow bell pepper
- **½** green bell pepper
- **10** green beans

For the sofrito
- **½ cup** olive oil
- **½** onion, thinly chopped
- **4** garlic cloves, thinly chopped
- **2** tomatoes, chopped
- Salt and pepper to taste

To serve (optional)
- **4 tbsp.** aioli
- **2** lemons
- Bread slices

Directions

Paella

In a paella pan, cook chicken cubes and chorizo with olive oil. Remove chicken and chorizo, but do not discard cooking oil. In the same paella pan, add rice, sofrito, and wine. Let simmer until white wine is reduced. Add lobster/shrimp stock, the chicken, chorizo, and baby back ribs. Season with salt and pepper. Once it comes to a boil, cover the pan and cook for 15 minutes. Season shrimp and calamari rings with salt and pepper. Add them to the rice with green peas and beans. Add mussels and bell pepper strips. Cover again and cook until all liquids are almost evaporated. Turn off the heat and let rest for 10 minutes before serving. If desired, accompany with bread slices, lemon wedges, and aioli.

Saffron-white wine and vegetables

Mix saffron with white wine and set aside. Cook bell peppers on the grill in order to peel them later. Once cooked, cut them in strips. In a pot with salted water, cook green beans. Strain and chill them in ice water.

Sofrito

Heat a sauté pan with olive oil. Cook chopped onions, garlic, and tomatoes. Season with salt and pepper.

YIELD
4 servings

PREP TIME
45 minutes

COOK TIME
30 minutes

DIFFICULTY
beginner

FRIED SHRIMP TACOS

by Chef Concepción Gonzaga

Ingredients

For the shrimp tempura
- **14 ounces (400 g)** 41/50 raw shrimp
- **12** corn tortillas
- **5 ¼ ounces (150 g)** flour for tempura
- **½ cup** water
- **1 quart (1l)** vegetable oil

For the habanero chili pepper dressing
- **2** habanero chili peppers
- **½** garlic clove
- **½ tablespoon** salt

- **2 tablespoons** white onion, chopped
- **4 tablespoons** water
- **10 ounces (300 g)** mayonnaise
- **6 tablespoons** sour orange juice

For the Mexican salsa
- **2.1 ounces (60 g)** tomato, chopped
- **1.4 ounces (40 g)** onion, chopped
- **1.4 ounces (40 g)** cilantro, chopped
- **.2 ounces (5 ml)** lime juice
- **¼ tablespoon** salt
- **1** serrano chili pepper, chopped

Directions

Shrimp tempura

Place flour in a bowl for the tempura. Add water and beat until a smooth consistency is formed with no lumps. Reserve and refrigerate. Heat the oil to medium temperature. Add salt and pepper to shrimp and drip in tempura paste. Fry until golden in color and drain on paper towels.

Habanero chili pepper dressing

Roast chili peppers in a sauté pan with garlic and onion. Once cooked, add water and process in blender. Add mayonnaise and orange juice. Blend thoroughly. Adjust seasoning with salt and reserve.

Mexican salsa (sauce)

In a bowl, add tomato, onion, cilantro, chili pepper and blend with lime juice. Season and reserve.

To serve

Heat the tortillas, and place about 3 to 4 shrimp in each one. Decorate with the Mexican salsa and a cilantro sprig. Accompany with the habanero pepper dressing and half a lime.

YIELD
4 servings

PREP TIME
1 hour

COOK TIME
35 minutes

DIFFICULTY
intermediate

SEA BASS FILET

by Chef Daniel Hernández

Ingredients

For the sea bass filets and sauce

- **Four 7 ounce (200-g)** sea bass filets
- **1** guajillo chili pepper, seeded
- **1** chilhuacle chili pepper, seeded
- **2** red onions
- **4** garlic cloves
- **4** Roma tomatoes
- **1** bay leaf
- **2** cumin seeds
- **2 cups** chicken stock
- **¼ cup** corn oil
- **1** banana leaf

To serve

- **2** limes
- **2 tablespoons** mayonnaise
- **4** cooked rice portions to taste
- **1** avocado, medium
- Salt and pepper to taste
- Edible flowers (optional)

Directions

Sea bass filets and sauce

Roast seeded chili peppers with 1 onion cut into 4 pieces and garlic cloves for 4 minutes. Add cut tomatoes, bay leaf, and cumin. Roast for 2 minutes more. Pour the chicken stock and simmer for 5 minutes, purée in a blender, and strain. Chop half an onion and sauté using half the oil, add puréed sauce, and simmer for 5 minutes. Season to taste. Cool the sauce over half of the banana leaf.

Sauce

Preheat the oven to 340 ˚F (170 ˚C). Season the filet with salt, pepper, and lime drops. Spread the mayonnaise on each filet and fully cover with the sauce. Cook in the oven for 12 minutes. With the remaining banana leaf, cut 4 rectangles, larger than the fish filet. Serve one filet on each rectangle and accompany with the rice. Garnish with sliced onion, lime wedges, and avocado pearls. If desired, serve with some sauce on the side.

Chef Daniel Hernández's Tip: It's better to cook the fish on the coal grill without removing scales to enhance the aroma.

EXECUTIVE CHEF, VIDANTA ACAPULCO

Daniel Hernández

He cooked rice for the first time when he was eight years old. That day, Daniel Hernández experienced the passion of creating and preparing a dish. After seeing the reactions on the faces of his family, he felt the satisfaction one gets from making people happy. In that very moment, he found the motivation to become what he is today, the Executive Chef at Vidanta Acapulco.

Daniel sees the creation of his main dishes and desserts like an architect building on a foundation of flavors. He almost always includes his favorite condiment, garlic, because of its health-promoting qualities. He knows that a dish is his letter of introduction and that the small details are very important. "What matters is to make the member feel that each meal is a unique moment," he maintains. In his private life, he likes traditional dishes, like "ranch-style" food, including "beans scented with epazote herb, chopped onions, cilantro, and chili pepper, served with fresh, hand-made tortillas."

*"Thanks to this profession, you
have the opportunity to cook for
former presidents, artists, singers,
politicians, and sports stars."*

TRY THIS DISH AT JOYÀ BY CIRQUE DU SOLEIL IN VIDANTA RIVIERA MAYA

DESSERTS

Recipe for Tropical Bread Pudding on page 73

YIELD
4 servings

PREP TIME
2 hours

BAKE TIME
20 minutes

DIFFICULTY
expert

PERFECT PASSION

by Chef Thierry Beuffe

Ingredients

For the Italian meringue
- **2 tbsp.** water
- **6.3 oz.** refined sugar
- **3.5 oz.** egg whites

For the passion fruit mousse
- **6.5 oz.** whipping cream
- **.7 oz.** gelatin sheets, hydrated
- **2.3 oz.** passion fruit purée
- **9.2 oz.** Italian meringue

For the raspberry pastry
- **2** eggs
- **.9 oz.** sugar
- **.7 oz.** raspberry purée
- **3 oz.** powdered sugar
- **2.1 oz.** ground almonds
- **.7 oz.** all-purpose flour
- **12** blueberries
- **4** spearmint leaves

To serve
- **24** raspberries
- **4 scoops** of ice-cream or sorbet
- **6** strawberries
- **1** kiwi

Directions

Italian meringue

Cook sugar until water reaches 250 °F (120 °C). In the meantime, beat the egg whites halfway through. Add cooked sugar to the whites gradually, and let cool in the medium-speed mixer.

Passion fruit mousse

Beat cream until it forms stiff peaks. Melt rehydrated gelatin and add to the warm passion fruit purée. Mix whipped cream with the pure gradually adding the Italian meringue. Fill a rectangular mold with the passion fruit mousse and add a couple of raspberries in the center. Cover with more mousse and freeze.

Raspberry pastry

Preheat oven to 320 °F (160 °C). Beat eggs, purée raspberries, and refined sugar until getting a meringue consistency. Sift powdered sugar, powder almonds, and flour. Gently add dry ingredients to the meringue, folding them in. Extend on a greased tray and bake for 8 minutes approximately.

To serve

Cut biscuit into rectangles a bit larger than the mousse mold. Take a biscuit rectangle, place mousse on top, and decorate with the fruit. Serve with ice-cream or sorbet on the side.

YIELD
4 servings

PREP TIME
1 hr. 30 mins.

BAKE TIME
45 minutes

DIFFICULTY
expert

GIANT MACARON

by Chef Thierry Beuffe

Ingredients

For the pastry cream
- **3 ½ ounces (100 ml)** milk
- **½** vanilla pod
- **2** egg yolks
- **1.8 ounces (50 g)** sugar
- **½ teaspoon** all-purpose flour
- **½ teaspoon** corn starch

For the light kirsch cream
- **200 g (7 oz)** pastry cream

- **1 tablespoon** kirsch brandy
- **2** gelatin sheets, softened in water
- **3 ½ ounces (100 g)** whipping cream

For the macaron
- **2.8 ounces (80 g)** powdered sugar
- **2. 8 ounces (80 g)** ground almonds

- **3 ounces (90 g)** egg whites
- **2.8 ounces (80 g)** refined sugar
- Red food color

For plating
- **32** raspberries
- **4 scoops** of raspberry sorbet
- **8** spearmint leaves
- **12** blueberries

Directions

Pastry cream

Boil milk with the vanilla pod cut in two. Beat yolks with sugar, flour, and corn starch. Add a dash of hot milk to the yolk mixture and return to the saucepan. Keep stirring continuously until it is a thick cream with no lumps. Cool.

Light kirsch cream

Whip pastry cream and heat to 86 °F (30°C). Add kirsch, melt gelatin and add it to the mixture. Fold in the whipping cream.

Giant macaron

Preheat oven to 275 °F (140 °C). Sift powdered sugar and ground almonds. Beat egg whites with sugar until stiff peaks are formed. Gently blend both mixtures until a soft consistency is obtained. Add some red color to get a pale pink color. On a tray with parchment paper, form eight circles, about 3 inches (8 cm) each, with the macaron mixture. Bake for 18 minutes.

To Serve

Using a pastry sleeve, fill the base of the macaron with the light cream, place the raspberries on top with some more light cream. Cover the second macaron. Decorate with the raspberries, blueberries, and spearmint leaves. Serve with a scoop of raspberry sorbet on the side.

YIELD
4 servings

PREP TIME
1 hour

BAKE TIME
30 minutes

DIFFICULTY
intermediate

TROPICAL BREAD PUDDING

by Chef Sergio Rios

Ingredients

For the bread pudding
- **2** eggs
- **6 oz.** whipping cream
- **6 oz.** coconut milk
- **2 oz.** brown sugar
- **1 tbs.** dark rum
- **4** pieces butter croissant, diced
- **1** ripe banana, diced
- **1 tsp.** natural vanilla extract
- **2 ½ oz.** caramel sauce

For the coconut streusel
- **3 oz.** all-purpose flour
- **2 oz.** finely grated dried coconut
- **1** pinch salt
- **2 oz.** white sugar
- **2 oz.** butter, softened

For the white chocolate ganache
- **2 oz.** white chocolate
- **1 ½ oz.** whipping cream

For the caramel sauce
- **1 tbs.** brown sugar
- **1 tbs.** glucose
- **1 tbs.** water
- **1 ½ oz.** whipping cream

Directions

Bread pudding
Combine caramel sauce with banana, mix, and place in pastry bag, allowing to cool at room temp. In a pan, warm up cream and coconut milk until it simmers, remove from heat. In a bowl, lightly whip egg, sugar, vanilla extract, and rum, whip inside cream and coconut milk, then incorporate croissant. Place mix in 4 silicon molds and pipe caramel-banana mix in center. Bake in a preheated oven at 350 °F for 30 minutes. Place in cooler for 1 hour.

Caramel sauce
In a pot, mix sugar, glucose, and water, then place over medium heat until caramel forms. Move from heat and whip cream until blended, then place aside.

Coconut streusel and white chocolate ganache
With an electric mixer, cream the butter and sugar, incorporate rest of ingredients until a flaky dough forms. Place in a paper-lined sheet pan and bake at 375 °F for 15 minutes, until golden-brown. Allow to cool, roughly chop, and set aside. For ganache, simmer cream in a pot, then remove from heat. In a bowl, place white chocolate pieces, incorporate warm cream and mix with a spoon until well blended. Put aside.

To serve
Remove bread pudding from cooler, and cover with warm ganache and coconut streusel. Place pudding on a plate, add a scoop of coconut ice cream on top. Chef recommends decorating with meringue chips and serving with a passion fruit sauce.

EXECUTIVE PASTRY CHEF, VIDANTA NUEVO VALLARTA

Thierry Beuffe

French-born Thierry Beuffe has traveled the world perfecting the techniques he uses to create the exquisite pastries at Vidanta Nuevo Vallarta, where members rave about his creations. Pastry making appealed to his artistic nature and his love of detail, even though he admits he does not have a sweet tooth. Adding innovative touches to simple recipes, he transforms desserts into sweet gems that reflect the world-famous pastries of his native France. His pastries have been savored by Robert De Niro and John Travolta, among other celebrities.

While he has extensive experience creating new delights and reimagining existing favorites, he also has a great respect for tradition. His main utensil is the paring knife, and his favorite ingredient, vanilla "because it is a very subtle flavor and goes well almost with everything." During his many travels, he has tried many desserts, but favors those "made with passion and superior ingredients." To those who want to devote their lives to pastry making, he offers some advice: "Learn everything you can and never stop learning, be patient, and do not skip any steps."

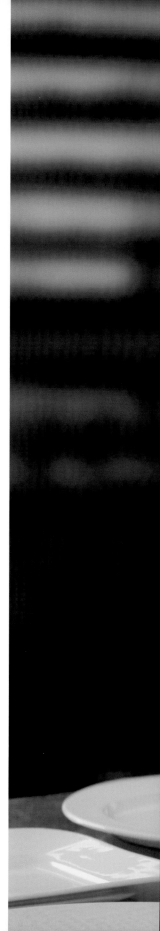

"I like making pastries because it is so focused on detail, so creative, so artistic."

TRY THIS COCKTAIL
AT SANTUARIO
AT VIDANTA
NUEVO VALLARTA

COCKTAILS

Recipe on page 89

Burke's Spring

YIELD
1 serving

PREP TIME
30 minutes

DIFFICULTY
intermediate

ALIX

by Luis Vicencio

A true gourmet cocktail, intense and passionate, this stands out among our select range of signature cocktails with its unique combination of Alix Garden tea and vodka. Adding red berries gives it a dazzling look.

Ingredients

For the cocktail

- **2 ½ ounces** Alix Garden tea
- **.4 oz (10 g)** raspberries
- **.4 oz (10 g)** blackberries
- **.3 ounces (10 ml)** lime juice
- **1 ounce (30 ml)** cranberry juice
- **½ oz (15 ml)** natural syrup
- **2 ounces (60 ml)** premium vodka
- **1** rosemary sprig

Directions

Method

Infuse the tea for 4 minutes in 10 ounces (300 ml) of hot water. Pour the Alix Garden tea and all the ingredients into a cocktail mixer, add ice, and shake intensely to blend the fruit properly. Serve in a tall glass with ice, decorate with a blackberry, a raspberry, and a rosemary sprig.

Tips from Luis Vicencio: *Use freshly prepared tea and freshly squeezed lime juice. Serve with crushed ice to maximize the cocktail's refreshing taste. This drink is a good pairing for salads, chicken, or grilled fish.*

YIELD
1 serving

PREP TIME
30 minutes

DIFFICULTY
intermediate

GRAND SPICE

by René Ramos

The Grand Spice is Mexican flavor in a glass. It has an amusing flavor with an acidic and spicy touch. This cocktail is the perfect marriage of Mexican tradition — chili pepper, tequila, and lime. When experienced together, they lift our spirit and tantalize our palate, filling us all with the soul of Mexico.

Ingredients

For the cocktail

- **2 ounces (60 ml)** white tequila (tequila blanca)
- **½ oz (15 g)** passion fruit pulp
- **1 ounce (30 ml)** lime juice
- **1 ounce (30 ml)** natural syrup
- **2 drops** Tabasco sauce
- **1** lime slice

Directions

Method

Put all the ingredients into a cocktail mixer, add ice, and shake. Strain and serve on the rocks using an Old-Fashioned glass. Add some Tabasco sauce drops and decorate with a slice of lime.

Tips from René Ramos: *Use fresh passion fruit to get the pulp and use only freshly squeezed lime juice.*

YIELD
1 *serving*

PREP TIME
30 minutes

DIFFICULTY
intermediate

MEZCALINA

by Modesto Güereña

Like Mexico, this cocktail is full of personality, spicy, traditional, with a smoky flavor at the same time. It is ideal to drink at daytime, preferably by the pool or with lunch.

Ingredients

For the cocktail

- **5** spearmint leaves
- **3** cucumber slices
- **2 ounces (60 ml)** of young mezcal
- **1 ounce (30 ml)** lime juice
- **½ ounce (15 ml)** natural syrup
- **½ tablespoon** worm salt (sal de gusano)

Directions

Method

Add spearmint and cucumber in a cocktail mixer, add mezcal and lime juice. Balance the mixture with natural syrup; add ice and shake vigorously. Circle the rim of a glass with worm salt and serve on the rocks. Decorate with cucumber slices.

Tips from Modesto Güereña: To ensure better flavor, use joven espadín mezcal and freshly squeeze the lime by hand. Pay attention to the freshness of the cucumber and spearmint to keep the drink from becoming bitter.

YIELD
1 serving

PREP TIME
30 minutes

DIFFICULTY
intermediate

THE GRAND COLLINS

by Luis Vicencio

Playing with innovative flavors using exotic fruits, herbs, and infusions is the new trend in signature cocktails. Achieving this perfect fusion, the Grand Collins has become an iconic cocktail at Vidanta.

Ingredients

For the hibiscus infusion

- **1.4 ounces (40 g)** dry hibiscus flowers
- **½ quart (½ l)** water
- **1½ pounds (700 g)** sugar

For the cocktail

- **2 ounces (60 ml)** premium vodka
- **1 ½ ounces (45 ml)** hibiscus flower infusion
- **1 ounce (30 ml)** lime juice
- **3** basil leaves
- Club soda to complete

Directions

Hibiscus flower infusion

Boil hibiscus in water until a ruby-red color is obtained. Strain out flowers and simmer to reduce. Add sugar gradually and keep cooking to achieve a syrupy consistency.

Beverage

Pour premium vodka in a cocktail mixer with ice. Add the hibiscus infusion, freshly squeezed lime juice, and basil leaf. Shake vigorously to extract oils from basil. Serve on the rocks. Add club soda and decorate with a basil leaf.

Tips from Luis Vicencio:
Hibiscus flower is key to this preparation. Be sure to select high quality flowers in order to get the expected color and flavors.

YIELD
1 serving

PREP TIME
30 minutes

DIFFICULTY
intermediate

TEMAZCAL COCKTAIL

by Rafael Ramos

It is as intense as a temazcal steam bath, but fresh as lime and spearmint. For those who enjoy subtle contrasts and the intense aromas of mezcal and fernet (Italian spirit), this cocktail is an elegant accompaniment to special moments. The added detail of a creamy and foamy topping will pleasantly surprise you.

Ingredients

For the cocktail

- **10** spearmint leaves
- **3 teaspoons** white sugar
- **¼ ounce** lime juice
- **6 drops** of fernet Branca
- **1 ounce (30 ml)** tequila reposado (aged tequila)
- **1 ounce (30 ml)** mezcal
- **1** egg white
- **2 ounces (60 ml)** club soda

Directions

Method

Soak seven spearmint leaves in sugar and lime juice in a cocktail mixer. Add ice, fernet Branca, aged tequila and mescal and shake. Pour the egg white and three spearmint leaves into a bowl. Beat until it has a foamy and consistent texture. Serve the cocktail in a martini glass and add club soda. Top it off with the egg white foam and let it float on the cocktail.

Tips from Rafael Ramos: *Prepare the foam at the end to maintain proper consistency when serving.*

YIELD
1 serving

PREP TIME
30 minutes

DIFFICULTY
intermediate

BURKE'S SPRING

by Luis Vicencio

This appealing cocktail entices you with the distinct aroma of bourbon mixed with scents of peach and mango. The artisanal syrup made from star anise, pink pepper, and a touch of vanilla creates a truly unique drink.

Ingredients

For artisanal syrup

- **12 ounces (350 ml)** water
- **2** star anise
- **5** pink peppercorns
- **½** vanilla pod
- **1 ½ pounds (650 g)** sugar

For the cocktail

- **1** pineapple slice
- **1** orange slice with peel
- **1 ounce (30 ml)** mango pulp
- **1 dash** lime juice
- **1 ounce (30 ml)** artisanal syrup
- **1 ½ ounces (45 ml)** bourbon
- **1 ounce (30 ml)** peach liquor
- **2** basil leaves

Directions

Artisanal syrup

Boil star anise, pepper, and vanilla in the water. Add sugar when it starts to boil. Let boil until it reaches a thick, syrupy consistency. Let cool.

Drink

Add the pineapple slice and the orange slice to cocktail mixer. Add mango pulp, a dash of lime juice, and the artisanal syrup. Add bourbon and peach liquor. Finally, add the basil leaf and ice. Shake vigorously. Serve on the rocks and decorate with a piece of pineapple.

Tips from Luis Vicencio: Pepper, star anise, and vanilla are strong flavor spices so it is important to watch the quantities when making the syrup. It should have a gentle, yet aromatic flavor.

BEVERAGE MANAGER, VIDANTA NUEVO VALLARTA

Luis Vicencio Curiel

Like any good Mexican, Luis Vicencio enjoys the traditions of his country, including a good mezcal and tequila, the country's signature liquors. "Personally, I like agave drinks, rich in flavors and aromas, going from citrus and herbal to more complex touches, such as wood, vanilla, and pepper. All from a single plant in comparison to vodkas or a whisky which can be made from a variety of grains or other ingredients," he explains.

Key to his profession is food and beverage pairing. "What matters most in a beverage is that it needs to be well-balanced in terms of sweetness and bitterness, so that each ingredient has something in common with others." He prefers classical drinks, but also likes to play with herbs and infusions. His personal philosophy: "You create – through charisma, originality, and style – the best cocktail for a member and become a friend to every visitor to our bar."

"I am passionate about cuisine and I love playing with aromas, flavors, textures, exotic fruit, and herb infusions of modern mixology."

SOMMELIER, VIDANTA RIVIERA MAYA

Ignacio Hernández

A good wine requires the right climate and soil to thrive and produce excellent quality grapes, such as Nebbiolo, the favorite grape of Vidanta Riviera Maya Sommelier Ignacio Hernández. According to him, a skilled sommelier has to have a good memory, speak three or more languages, and use a clear way of speaking when presenting a new wine to a guest. "Be humble and sincere when teaching what you know," he says.

For almost 15 years, Ignacio has been sharing his passion and love for wine with members in the Vidanta restaurants, enriching Vidanta's wine cellars and conducting tastings and seminars, where he shows members how to discover the differences that "can be figured out by using the right tasting techniques." A knowledgeable sommelier, he has tasted wines in Bordeaux with noted experts such as Stèphane Derenoncourt, a leader in biodynamic winemaking, and pays homage to Michel Rolland, one of the most significant wine gurus in the world. But he offers a very basic philosophy about his work: "A sommelier needs to study a lot, but above all, has to be aware of the fact that learning in this world never ends. One must be willing to search for as much knowledge as possible."

"Being able to share knowledge with younger generations interested in this wonderful world of wine tasting has been my best reward as a wine specialist."

VIDANTA LOS CABOS

VIDANTA PUERTO PEÑASCO

VIDANTA MAZATLÁN

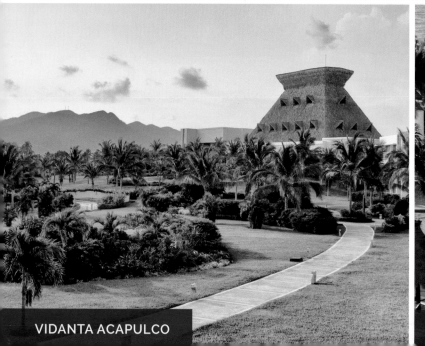

VIDANTA ACAPULCO

VIDANTA RIVIERA MAYA